COYOTE
MOON

Maria Gianferrari

Pictures by
Bagram Ibatoulline

Roaring Brook Press
New York

Moon rises as Coyote wakes in her den,
a hollowed-out pine in a cemetery.
Coyote crawls between roots.
She sniffs the air, arches her back,
shakes her fur.

Pups peek through the roots' fingers.
It's nighttime in the neighborhood,
and Coyote's family is hungry.

Pups wait near the den.
They're easy prey for swooping hawks,
but their older siblings stand by as sentinels.

Coyote trots along roads,
under fences, between houses.
She slips through the night
as quiet as a ghost, searching for prey.

Coyote listens.

Her triangle ears sit high on her head.

She hears scratching.

She slides through boxwood, then crouches.

POUNCE!

Mouse scuttles.
Coyote digs and digs,
but Mouse is safe
beneath the stone wall.

Coyote sniffs.
She creeps through tangled brush,
tracking the scent of golf-course Geese.
She follows her nose,
then lurks among alder bushes.

Coyote charges the nest.
Geese hiss and dive,
honk and snap,
nipping Coyote's back.
Coyote flees.
No eggs for breakfast.

Coyote looks.
Her sharp eyes spy Rabbit.
She slinks, silent as a shadow.

Twigs crack.
Rabbit freezes.
Ears twitch.
Coyote lunges.
Rabbit leaps.
Shadows blur.
Coyote is fast, but Rabbit is faster,
skittering under the slide to safety.

The moon sinks.
Stars fade from the sky.
The sun's eye peeks.

Coyote threads through rusty reeds.
At the fringe where earth and water meet,
she wades, and waits.

Coyote hears gobbling.
Coyote smells droppings.
Coyote sees Turkey
unfurling his feathers like a fan.
Turkey struts,
drumming and dragging his wings.
Coyote springs.

Now Coyote's family will eat.

Coyote drops Turkey to sing
"Yeeeep-yip-yip-yoooo" to the dawn.

"Yeeeep!"
"Yip-yip-yip-yip!"
"Yoooo!"
Coyote's family sings back.

You open your window.
Coyote hears, sniffs, looks.
You watch as Coyote slips under
the fence painted pink by the sun.

Beyond your backyard, past the fence, by the cemetery,
Coyote's family feasts.

Full-bellied, they will sleep.
Until the moon wakes them again.

COYOTE FACTS

HOME SWEET HOME

Coyotes live in dens. They dig multiple sites (equipped with emergency exits) and sometimes use the abandoned dens of other animals. They prefer to live in edge habitats, which are wooded areas bordering fields. Trees and shrubbery provide cover for hunting. In the suburbs, where this story takes place, a golf course or cemetery becomes an ideal hunting ground.

TERRITORY

Coyotes have sniffed their way into cities and suburbs in their search for food and new territory. Territory is an area that an animal defends. Coyotes keep nonfamily members off their turf by marking their borders with urine and scat.

Coyotes live in every American state except Hawaii. They range as far north as Alaska and as far south as Panama and live in a variety of habitats: woodlands, wetlands, deserts, grasslands, and tundras. They even live in large cities. In the spring of 2015, several were spotted around New York City—one was seen on a rooftop in Queens! When caught, they're released in the wild.

PLAYFUL PUPS

While parents hunt, pups wait, but they're not alone. Last year's pups—their older siblings—help guard the den. Coyote pups are like kids: they play hide-and-seek, tag, and tug-of-war. By playing games, pups practice how to hunt and how to escape from predators.

OLYMPIC ATHLETES

Coyotes are like long jumpers, leaping up to twelve feet to pounce on prey. They are also sprinters, running as fast as forty miles an hour in a chase. Their tails act as rudders, helping them turn.

FAST FOOD

Coyotes are thriving because they have been able to adapt their diet to their surroundings. They aren't picky eaters; they're opportunistic. That means they eat what's available. Eighty percent of the coyote's diet includes rabbits as well as rodents such as mice, rats, and voles, but they also eat other kinds of food, depending on their habitat and the season. In the desert, prickly pears and lizards are on the menu. Rats and garbage are city fare for coyotes. In the winter tundra, coyotes eat hare and deer. In summer, coyotes eat watermelons and berries, as well as grasshoppers, beetles, and grubs. Coyotes also control the population of Canada geese by eating their eggs.

CANINE COMMUNICATION

Coyotes howl, growl, bark, wail, and squeak. The coyote's Latin name is *Canis latrans*, or barking dog. Scientists have observed that coyotes use many distinctive sounds to communicate with one another.

CANINE COUSINS

There are two main types of coyotes in North America: the eastern coyote and the western coyote. Historically, coyotes and wolves were natural enemies who competed for similar food sources. However, the consequences of European settlement in the eastern part of North America—namely deforestation, hunting, and poisoning—caused the wolf population to be severely reduced. With fewer wolves around, more coyotes moved into wolf territory, and the remaining wolves began to view them as potential mates rather than enemies. Scientists now know that the eastern coyote is actually a coywolf hybrid, larger than its western cousin. The origins of the first coywolf have been traced to Algonquin Park in Ontario, Canada, in 1919.

How are western coyotes and eastern coyotes (coywolves) different? Coywolves have longer legs, bigger paws and skulls, shorter snouts, smaller ears, and bushier tails than western coyotes. The coyotes in this book are eastern coyotes.

FURTHER READING

Mattern, Joanne. *Coyotes.* North Mankato, Minn.: Capstone Press, 2012.

Read, Tracy C. *Exploring the World of Coyotes.* Buffalo, N.Y.: Firefly Books, 2011.

Swanson, Diane. *Coyotes.* Milwaukee: Whitecap Books, 2011.

Swinburne, Stephen R. *Coyote: North America's Dog.* Honesdale, Pa.: Boyds Mills Press, 2007.

Winner, Cherie. *Coyotes.* Minneapolis: Carolrhoda Books, 1995.

WEBSITES

Coywolf Video: pbs.org/wnet/nature/coywolf-meetthecoywolf/8605

Eastern Coyote/Coywolf Research: easterncoyoteresearch.com

The Humane Society of the United States: humanesociety.org/animals/coyotes

Project Coyote: projectcoyote.org

Urban Coyote Research: urbancoyoteresearch.com

In memory of my aunt Marie, aka Ree Ree, a survivor, like the coyote
—M.G.

To Doktor Henri Robcis
—B.I.

Text copyright © 2016 by Maria Gianferrari
Illustrations copyright © 2016 by Bagram Ibatoulline
Published by Roaring Brook Press
Roaring Brook Press is a division of Holtzbrinck Publishing Holdings Limited Partnership
175 Fifth Avenue, New York, New York 10010
mackids.com

Library of Congress Cataloging-in-Publication Data
Gianferrari, Maria, author.
    Coyote moon / Maria Gianferrari ; pictures by Bagram Ibatoulline.
    pages cm
    Summary: "A nonfiction picture book about coyotes hunting in suburban neighborhoods at night."—
Provided by publisher.
    Audience: Ages 4–8.
    ISBN 978-1-62672-041-1 (hardcover)
    1. Coyote—Juvenile literature.   2. Urban animals—Juvenile literature.   I. Ibatoulline, Bagram,
illustrator.   II. Title.

QL737.C22G5195 2016
599.77'25—dc23

2015012694

Our books may be purchased in bulk for promotional, educational, or business use. Please contact your local bookseller or the
Macmillan Corporate and Premium Sales Department at (800) 221-7945 ext. 5442 or by e-mail at MacmillanSpecialMarkets@macmillan.com.

First edition 2016
Book design by Andrew Arnold
Color separations by Bright Arts (H.K.) Ltd.
Printed in China by Toppan Leefung Printing Ltd., Dongguan City, Guangdong Province

1 3 5 7 9 10 8 6 4 2